Bears
of the World

Bear mothers have a close relationship with their cubs, as well as being protective of them.

Bears
of the World

Dorothy Hinshaw Patent

Holiday House, New York

Library of Congress Cataloging in Publication Data

Patent, Dorothy Hinshaw.
  Bears of the world.

  Bibliography: p.
  Includes index.
  SUMMARY: Dicusses the behavior and physical characteristics of the seven species of bears, the mysteries of
bear hibernation, the relationship between bears and
humans throughout history, and the need to understand,
protect, and live with bears.
  1. Bears—Juvenile literature. [1. Bears] I. Ti-
tle.
QL737.C27P36   599'.74446   79-23149
ISBN 0-8234-0409-9

*For Chuck Jonkel and other bear researchers
who are trying to save bears
and, along with them, some wilderness for the future.*

ACKNOWLEDGMENTS

I wish to thank
Doctors Charles Jonkel, E. W. Pfeiffer, Ralph Nelson, and
Philip Wright for their help with this book.

Contents

One • Bears Will Be Bears, 13

Two • Our Most Familiar Bear, 25

Three • Our Magnificent Grizzly and Its Kin, 37

Four • Giant of the North, 58

Five • The Rest of the Family, 71

Six • The Mysteries of Winter Sleep, 85

Seven • Bears and People, 94

Eight • Living with Bears, 103

Suggested Reading, 119

Index, 123

Bears
of the World

When bears sit up and beg for food, as this South American spectacled bear is doing, one tends to think of them as cute, tame animals.

One

Bears Will Be Bears

Bears are among our most familiar animals. Many children take a teddy bear to bed for company at night, and most people have heard of Smokey the Bear, with his friendly pointers about fire in the forest. Everyone has some idea of what a bear is. But our feelings about bears are very mixed up. On the one hand, we think of bears as soft, cuddly, somewhat amusing animals. When we see a bear begging for food in the zoo, we think how cute it looks. And if a bear should be standing by the highway when we are driving through a park, chances are we will stop the car for a closer look. Many people even get out of their cars and feed the bears by hand, as if they had nothing to fear from Smokey's cousin. But people also fear the "killer grizzly." They are terrified of meeting up with a grizzly while hiking in Yellowstone or Glacier Park. Hollywood encourages this idea by making films of grizzlies ruthlessly ripping people apart.

Whatever their opinion of bears, people have been

fascinated by them since they were first encountered. Humans tend to feel a kinship with bears. Familiar bears are often about the size of a person. They can stand on their hind legs like a human; they may use their front paws like hands; and they eat much the same foods as we do. For these reasons, people have often considered bears as "brothers," or ancestors, in myths and stories.

Like prehistoric humans, bears often inhabited caves. For this reason and because of their similar diets, people and bears must often have come in contact with one another. Compared to a bear, a human was weak. While people had to live in groups to survive, bears could make it on their own very easily. The strength and independence of bears have inspired human respect over

Bears have short tails and stocky legs. Here is an Alaskan brown bear with her cubs. MICHAEL LUQUE

the ages. Bears have been admired and worshiped in many cultures, and bear worship lasted even into the twentieth century among some Japanese tribes. The images of bears as either cute or vicious are actually rather recent ideas based more on fantasy than on fact. Because most modern Americans live in cities, far from the forests and northern wastelands where bears thrive, we have lost the feeling for bears as the strong, intelligent, wild animals they really are.

Traits in Common

The seven different bear species share many traits. All are large animals. Male polar and Alaskan brown bears may weigh more than three-quarters of a ton and reach a height of over three meters (ten feet) tall when standing on their hind feet. Even the smallest, the Malayan sun bear, sometimes gets to be as heavy as a person, weighing as much as 65 kilograms (144 pounds). All bears have short, thick legs, heavy bodies, and strong, muscular necks. They walk flat-footed like humans instead of running on their toes like dogs, cats, and horses. They have very short tails which are barely noticeable and rather small, rounded ears. While their small eyes do not see very well, their noses are very sensitive. A bear's fur is usually fairly uniform in color, but several kinds may have light-colored patches on their chests. These probably serve to accent the bear's size when it stands up on its hand legs to defend itself. The spectacled bear has light circles around its eyes in addition to a light chest patch.

The bears' "secret of success" may lie in their diet, for bears will eat just about anything they can get their paws on. Far from being great killers, most bears are mainly plant eaters. They also eat small animals and feed on the carcasses of large animals which have died of starvation or disease. Some bears eat more meat than others. The polar bear, for example, is a superb seal hunter. But even polar bears know how to take advantage of an opportunity; once 42 of these solitary hunters were seen gathered around the carcass of a dead whale. The sloth bear has its own rather unique method of feeding by digging up termite nests with its sharp claws and sucking up the inhabitants with its flexible lips.

In the fall, most bears become very hungry and eat almost continuously. For twenty hours a day, the black bear eats. It wolfs down three times as much food as it usually does and gains more than a hundred pounds. Bears especially enjoy feasting on ripe berries, and human huckleberry pickers in the western mountains must keep a lookout to make sure they aren't taking over the favorite patch of a local black or grizzly bear. Bears need to fatten up in the fall because they spend the winter resting in their protected dens, sleeping most of the winter away.

All bears eat a varied diet. This spectacled bear is enjoying an ear of corn.

American Bears

The most familiar bears are the North American ones —the black bear, the grizzly bear, and the polar bear. The first of these has an unfortunate common name, for all "black bears" are not black. The black bear is called by scientists *Ursus americanus.* This scientific name, written in the Latin language, means simply "American bear" All "black bears," no matter what color they are, belong to this scientific species. Black bears may be black, brown, or even white. But whatever their color, they are still called black bears.

The grizzly belongs to a different bear species named *Ursus arctos.* When the grizzly was first studied by biologists, they thought it was a separate species and gave it the name *Ursus horribilis,* or "horrible bear." You can see that the grizzly has had its bad reputation for a long time. Now the grizzly is considered as just one variety of "brown" bear, along with the Asian and European brown bears and the Alaskan brown bears. "Brown bear" is also a confusing name, for brown bears come in several colors, ranging from cream to black. The grizzly got its common name from the gray-tipped fur found on many individuals (grizzled means partly gray).

Polar bears live in the icy cold Arctic areas all around the north pole. **Polar bears are almost pure white in** winter, changing to a creamy yellow color during the summer. Alaska is the only state in the United States where polar bears live. They have very special characteristics which enable them to thrive in such a harsh land, and scientists are carefully studying them to see what can be learned about how animals survive in extreme environments.

Other Bears

Not only are the North American bears the most familiar to us, they are also the ones best studied by

Even in the same family, "brown" bears may vary in color. These three Alaskan brown bears are waiting for their mother to bring them some fresh salmon from the McNeil River.

MICHAEL LUQUE

Is the giant panda a bear? While many scientists believe it is, others feel that it is more closely related to the lesser panda, shown here. The lesser panda is more like a raccoon than a bear.

scientists. Little is known about the four other kinds—the South American spectacled bear, the Asiatic black bear, the Malayan sun bear, and the Indian sloth bear. You may have seen some of these bears in the zoo. Most of them live in hard-to-reach areas where few biologists work.

Many experts also put the giant panda into the bear family. Other scientists place pandas in the raccoon family, and still others solve the problem by inventing a new family just for the pandas. The problem is that there are two kinds of pandas. The giant panda, which is the familiar big black-and-white one, looks very much like a bear. But the smaller lesser panda, which most scientists agree is closely related to the giant species, is more raccoon-like in its traits.

How Bears Came to Be

Although they feed on a variety of foods, bears belong to the biological family named the Carnivora, or meat eaters. Their distant ancestors were small, meat-eating

The giant panda, with its stocky body and short tail, certainly looks like a bear. Inside, as well as outside, it has many similarities to bears.

SCHROEDER EASTWOOD/NATIONAL ZOOLOGICAL PARK

tree climbers called miacids, which lived many millions of years ago. Because fossils of miacids are quite rare, scientists do not know the details of how they evolved into modern carnivores. But early on, two separate groups of carnivores developed. One was the cat group. The other was the dog group. Bears, weasels, and raccoons, as well as dogs and their relatives, form the dog branch of the family. The earliest bears were much smaller than most kinds living today. They lived in European forests over three million years ago. Most bears of today are closely related to one another and have evolved from the same prehistoric species, the Etruscan bear. Just where the spectacled bear fits in, however, is still uncertain. It is clearly different in many ways from other bears.

The different bear species apparently evolved in the Old World. The Asiatic black bear of today is much like its Etruscan ancestor, and our American black bear probably evolved from an early type of Asiatic black bear. Brown bears also developed from the Etruscan species. One brown bear, the cave bear, is now extinct. Cave bears lived in the time of prehistoric people. These bears had huge heads and grew even bigger than the largest bears alive today. Some people think that cavemen worshiped the cave bear because bear bones found in some European caves seem to have been carefully arranged. But other experts say that the evidence of bear worship is actually very slight. They point out that the bones could have been pushed around by cave animals over thousands of years. While some experts think that people had something to do with the extinction of the cave bears, most believe that humans were not involved.

The brown bear of today evolved in northern areas where there was much open space. Several features—their large size and their aggressiveness, for example—seem to be related to living in more open areas. The polar bear, which has completely adapted to living in treeless northern regions, seems to have developed relatively recently from brown bears. The polar bear has come the farthest from the forest-dwelling Etruscan bear. Most places where polar bears are found are completely treeless.

Bear Family Life

While they can tolerate one another if necessary, adult bears are basically solitary animals. During the spring mating season, males and females may stay together for a time. But the rest of the year, male bears keep to themselves. After mating, the female bear goes her own way, too. The sperm from the male bear fertilize from one to four (rarely more) tiny egg cells in the female's body. These fertilized eggs divide a few times to form microscopic embryos which float around in the womb, or uterus, of the female bear. The embryos of most mammals soon become attached to the wall of the uterus and rapidly grow into fetuses. But bear embryos stop developing when still just clusters of cells. Only in late fall do these tiny embryos finally become attached to the uterine wall and develop further. Some biologists believe that this slowing of development, called "delayed implantation," helps control bear populations. If a female bear cannot find enough food during the fall, the embryos may not develop at all. Then the female would not have to devote any of her limited reserves to developing cubs.

Baby bears are born in a den during the coldest, darkest time of winter. They are very small and helpless when born, but become much bigger and stronger before leaving the den. Mother bears take such good care of their cubs that few die while under their care. The mothers nurse the babies and teach them how to hunt. They protect them from enemies and show them how to avoid danger. Young bears stay with their mothers for at least several months. Some kinds leave only after 2½ or 3 years. When they do finally take off on their own, the cubs often stick together for a few more months. Then the essentially solitary nature of the bear takes over, and each young one goes its own way.

Two

Our Most Familiar Bear

When white settlers came to our east coast from Europe, they soon encountered bears. European bears are brown, but this new bear was a glossy black, so naturally they called it the "black bear." As explorers, trappers, and then settlers moved westward across the country in the 17th and 18th centuries, they found brown, blonde, and reddish brown black bears; black bears with black and white hairs mixed; black bears with white marks on their chests; and even white "black bears." Naturally, they thought they were seeing more than one kind of bear. Even today, many people think that bears such as the "cinnamon bear" are different from the black kind. But actually, all of these differently colored bears belong to the species officially known as the "American black bear" (*Ursus americanus*).

The confusion about color is only one of the misunderstandings people have about our most familiar bear. Because it is so familiar to us in the wild, as "Smokey the Bear," as the begging zoo bear, and as the

This black bear (Ursus americanus) *in Montana is wearing an ear tag. The activities of tagged bears can be followed by scientists so that more can be learned about how bears live.*

"cute cub" in Hollywood films, we think we know something about it. Actually, biologists have only seriously studied black bears for the last 20 years or so, and wildlife departments at colleges and universities have not considered the black bear as a particularly important species until fairly recently.

Bears are especially difficult animals to study. Because they are large, strong, and sometimes aggressive, they cannot easily be kept in laboratories for experiments. They live in rugged forests, are generally secretive, and are often active mainly at night. They live alone and may range over large areas. For all these reasons, it takes years of patient and expensive research to find out much about these interesting but elusive animals.

Designed for the Woods

We do know many things about black bears, however. For example, black bears may look like awkward, bumbling creatures, but their appearance is deceiving. A black bear can easily outrun a person, and it can shinny up a tree trunk with amazing ease. Their powerful build allows bears to break through the forest underbrush effortlessly. They can rear up on their hind legs to a height of about two meters (over six feet) to see over bushes. Their sharp claws are narrow and curved, which makes them useful in climbing. A black bear can bend its front claws downward so that they almost touch the foot pad. This allows the bear to grasp objects firmly and flip them over in search of food. Black bears use their powerful front paws to subdue prey, and they can easily kill a small creature such as an elk calf with one casual blow.

While bears have a reputation for poor eyesight,

black bears at least appear to have good close-up vision. They can sort out small bits of food such as berries and eat them, and they can carefully pick out small insects or scattered acorns on the forest floor. Their ability to see colors helps them distinguish objects at close range. Their hearing is also good (some have very large, mule-like ears), and their sense of smell is especially keen. Black bears can detect the odor of a dead animal from far off and find their way to the carcass directly.

Black bear young are born in the deep of winter, inside the dark den their mother chose in the fall. While the mother is considerably heavier than a big human, the newborn cub, only 20 centimeters (8 inches) long and weighing only about a half a kilogram (one pound), is closer in size to a rat than to a newborn person. It is almost helpless, with sparse black fur, closed eyes, and undeveloped ears. It can do little more than find one of its mother's nipples and begin to suck her nourishing milk.

Bear milk is very rich. It contains 25 to 33% fat, while cow's milk averages only about 3% fat. Bear milk also contains plenty of protein, but sugar, an important ingredient in cow's milk, is present in only minute quantities. The tiny young bears need this concentrated food to help them grow strong enough to leave the den by springtime.

Why do bears have such small babies, smaller than those of any other mammals except kangaroos and their

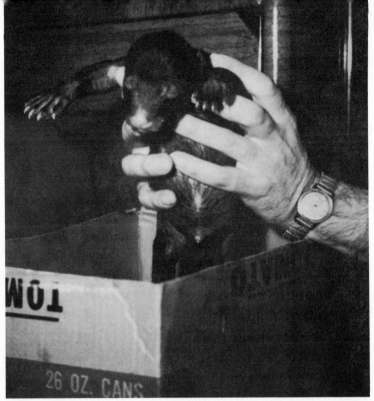

While an adult female black bear weighs around 125 kilograms (275 pounds), her cubs are very small and undeveloped when born. This cub is less than a month old. Its eyes are still closed and its ears are still undeveloped.

relatives? We are not sure, but the birth process itself is easy with small babies, and therefore not a danger during the mother bear's winter inactivity. And, since she must nurse her young for three or four months before food becomes abundant, the mother bear could hardly nourish two or three large offspring adequately.

As the cubs grow, they begin to look more bear-like. They sprout a fine, downy black coat by the time they are a couple of weeks old. When they are 40 or so days old, they open their eyes, and their first sharp, little teeth emerge. While they are now about 30 centimeters (one foot) long and weigh about a kilogram (around two pounds), the cubs are still quite weak and helpless. They can move only slowly, often pulling themselves along with their forelegs while dragging their still-weak hing legs behind. In their movements, they tend to crawl around in a circle; they never seem to get anywhere. These weak muscles and this tendency to go around in circles probably help protect the little bears from straying out of the den before the proper time; moving in a circle always brings them back to mother.

With the melting snows of spring comes time to leave the den. Male bears tend to be the first to come out, while females with cubs venture forth later. Bears in northern areas tend to stay in their dens later than those farther south, since winter's cold lasts longer there. When the mother finally leaves the den with her cubs, they have grown many times in size, but they are still small even by human baby standards. They weigh about 2¼ to 4½ kilograms (5 to 10 pounds) and have thick coats. Their claws are well developed, and one of the first things they learn to do is to climb, and climb fast. When danger threatens, the mother bear chases her cubs up the nearest tree, where they will be safe from danger. Strangely enough, the only real enemies of bears other than humans are other bears. Large male black bears and grizzly bears may attack and kill cubs, so it is important for the young animals to be able to scramble quickly up a tree and climb out to the farthest branches.

Shortly after leaving the den, the mother bear sheds her warm winter coat, leaving a thinner coat for the warm summer ahead. By the next fall, she will grow a new, thick coat to keep her warm. Food is scarce in

This fuzzy little bear cub is about four months old. He looks much more bearlike than he did when he was born, but he will need the watchful care of his mother for a long time.

CHARLES JONKEL

early spring, and bears tend to lose weight during the first weeks out of the den. They eat fresh grasses, herbs, and tender twigs, and may be lucky enough to find the carcass of a deer or elk which starved during the winter. But it may be several weeks before the bears are able to gain weight.

Early Family Life

The cubs go everywhere with their mother. They learn from her the many secrets of bear life, such as where the best fishing stream is. She nourishes them with her milk and protects them from dangerous adult male bears. Play is very important to young bears. The cubs play "chasing and fighting" games, much like puppies. One cub will sneak up on another and give a painful nip on the flank, then race off while the second cub chases furiously behind. Sometimes these chases move into the trees, giving the cubs a chance to practice their tree-climbing skills. In play fighting, one cub will come up to the other, rear up and paw at it, and a fight is on. The cubs may stand up and push at each other, trying to knock one another off balance. If one cub is down, the other may grab its neck between its teeth while the captured cub claws madly with its hind legs in an effort to free itself. If the play gets too rough, one cub will break it off by flattening his ears and perhaps letting out a low warning sound. If this doesn't end the roughhousing, a quick and painful bite does the trick. Other than the warning sounds which end play, bears are silent while playing. Cubs may induce their mothers to play, too, and young bears as old as four years old may indulge extensively in fun and games now and then.

As the cubs grow, they learn how to dig for ants and termites, and how to get honey from a beehive. By the time they are about seven months old, they are weaned and no longer feed on their mother's milk. In some rare cases, however, female black bears have nursed their young for more than a year, especially high in the mountains where the summer season is short.

As fall approaches, the bear family spends more and more time eating. Berries ripen and bears gorge themselves. Pine nuts and acorns are nourishing fall food, and the bears never seem to get their fill. They eat and eat and then eat more. They store a thick layer of fat on their bodies, which is vital to their survival through the winter. Not only does the fat provide energy for the bears during their four to six months of winter sleep, it also helps insulate their bodies and hold in warmth during the cold winter. In October or November, black bears den. They choose a dry, protected site such as a natural cave, or a hollow at the base of a tree. A few black bears dig their dens, chosing a spot under the roots of a large tree or under a rotting log where the entrance is protected. In areas of mild climate, where the big trees have been logged out, bears may simply den in a ground bed among dense vegetation. Some black bears, especially females, rake soft leaves and other debris into their nests to lie on.

The mother and her cubs curl up together in their den, but males and young independent females den alone. Black bears sleep through the winter even in areas with mild climates. Along the coast of the state of Washington, it rarely freezes in the winter, and frequent rainfall results in thriving plant growth. But even there, black bears enter their dens in October or November and do not come out again until the end of March.

Although their heartbeat slows and their body temperature lowers slightly, bears in winter sleep are easily aroused. If danger should threaten, such as a hunting wolf pack or a band of hunters out for winter meat, the sleeping bear can awaken rapidly and defend itself very effectively. Sometimes, when disturbed by curious scientists, bears have left their winter dens and found new, possibly less disturbed places to spend the winter.

Time for Independence

Usually in April, the mother and cubs emerge from the den to begin a new "bear year." But this one will be different for all of them, for by June, the mother may be ready to mate. At this time, the young bears are forced out on their own. The female loses interest in them, and the nearness of a male bear is clearly dangerous for the cubs. So they depart to begin life on their own. The cubs may stay together for as long as a year, or they may go their separate ways from the start.

Life is not easy for the young bears out on their own. They are still small enough to be attacked by adult males, and if they come across an abundant source of food such as a garbage dump, they must give way first to older bears before daring to take their share. But they learn their mother's lessons well in food finding and avoiding trouble, and most bear cubs survive to adulthood.

Bears take a long time to become adults. In some areas, female bears are ready to mate when they are 3½ years old. If such a young female mates successfully, she is likely to have only one cub the first time. Later on, she may possibly have as many as five or six babies, but litters of two are most common. Where food is abundant, female bears usually have a new family every two years until they die. In zoos, bears can live to be 40 years old, but in the wild they usually die at a much younger age. Any bear over 20 years old in the wild is very old.

In the north, where the growing season for plants is short, black bears may reproduce very slowly. In the Big Creek area of Montana, near Glacier National Park, females do not mate until they are 4½ years or more old, and are not likely to mate successfully before they are 6½. The bears are smaller there than elsewhere, and females breed less often and have smaller litters than in less harsh regions.

Bears tend to wander over quite large areas during

their lives, but they usually stay in one particular vicinity. During the year, a black bear may range over an area of 15 square miles or more, but it will not leave this familiar region. Male bears wander more than females. Young bears, especially males in search of permanent home areas, may end up many miles from where they were raised. Part of a bear's range includes areas it shares with other bears, where food is available only part of the year. Mountain slopes, which during most of the year do not provide much food, may be loaded with juicy, nourishing berries during the late summer. Several bears from surrounding areas may all feed together in such an area.

One mystery of bear behavior is the scratching up of certain tree trunks. Some biologists think that these are "signposts" made by resident bears, telling any strange bears that might wander through that the area is already taken. But other scientists do not agree and feel that bears do not mark their home areas in any way. Whatever their purpose, the trees are scratched diligently by bears, and they are very interesting and puzzling for humans to observe.

Three

Our Magnificent Grizzly
and Its Kin

The brown bear was once one of the widest-ranging animals known. It lived over most of Europe, in Asian mountains, across the forests of Canada, in the western United States, and even in Mexico. With the advance of civilization, the range of the brown bear has shrunk until it has become largely a bear of northern, wild regions—a symbol of wildness in an increasingly tame world. The California grizzly disappeared around 1924, and a few animals may survive in the Mexican mountains. Of all brown bears, the American grizzly is the most familiar to us. It is also probably the most dramatic of brown bears, for it is among the largest and most aggressive varieties. Fortunately, it is also the best known, thanks largely to the studies of Dr. Frank Craighead and his brother, Dr. John Craighead. The Craigheads and their co-workers studied the grizzly in Yellowstone Park, beginning in 1959 and, unfortunately, ending in 1971. They pioneered the use of radio for tracking animals and learned much about the habits of these elusive animals.

How to Track a Grizzly

Studying wild bears takes a lot of hard work. The animals must be trapped and tagged so that the movements of individual animals can be followed. Measurements of the bears must also be taken, not an easy task when you are dealing with hundreds of pounds of unconscious animal which may wake up before you are done. But tagging and measuring gives only some information. In order to understand the animal's movements from day to day, random sightings are not enough. The scientists must be able to track down a particular individual when they want to. Then they can find out just when the bear takes off for a particular feeding area, and how far it travels on a given day. And if they can follow an individual animal, they have some chance of tracking it to its winter den.

The Craigheads and their co-workers were the first to

Biologist Chris Serveen removes a dart from an unconscious 227-kilogram (500-pound) grizzly bear (Ursus arctos). The dart injected a measured dose of anesthetic so that scientists could take measurements of the bear and tag it for further study.

BORDER GRIZZLY PROJECT

carry on research using radio-collared bears. The collar, which was slipped onto a bear's neck while it was unconscious, had a radio transmitter with batteries. It was coated with paraffin and silicone rubber to make it waterproof, and covered with a strong acrylic resin to protect it from damage. The inside of the collar was padded so that it fit the bear comfortably but snugly, The transmitter would send out a signal of beeps which came at precise intervals. Each collar had a different beeping frequency so that the signals from different bears could be distinguished. A laboratory was set up in the park where tracking equipment picked up the signals from the bears. The bears could be tracked day and night, and the equipment could pick up signals from miles away. When the researchers wanted to follow a particular bear, they would take to the field with a hand-held receiver. This receiver had a loop-shaped antenna. By turning the antenna, the scientists could determine the direction where the signal was strongest, indicating the bear's location.

With time, these determined biologists learned how to interpret the radio signals. If a bear was actively moving around, its signal would vary in strength as it passed through the trees and changed direction. A constant signal not varying in loudness meant the bear was resting or sleeping. A signal which came and went usually meant that the bear was on the move. The signal died out when the animal passed over a hill or into very dense timber, and came back again when it was in the open. Since the equipment could follow several bears at one time, a great deal of information was obtained about grizzly behavior.

Introducing the Grizzly

The grizzly bear is superbly adapted to its wilderness life. Grizzlies are very large bears. Females usually weigh about 300 pounds, but mature males may tip the scales at over a half ton. Grizzlies differ from their black bear cousins in several ways. The grizzly face has a flattened, saucerlike look, while the black bear's face is more elongated. Grizzlies have a pronounced shoulder hump which black bears lack. Black bear claws are curved and sharp, adapted for climbing trees. Grizzly claws are thicker and straighter, powerful digging tools. While black bear claws do not show on its tracks, grizzly claws may dig deep into the ground as the animal walks.

Grizzlies vary widely in color and markings. While they are usually brown, black and light-colored individuals are also common. Some grizzlies, especially when young, have collars of light fur around their necks. And, of course, many individuals sport the light-tipped long guard hairs which give the animal its common names—grizzly, silvertip, and white bear.

Grizzlies will eat just about anything. They lie in

During the springtime, grizzlies feed on grass in mountain meadows. The prominent shoulder hump and short muzzle characteristic of grizzlies can be seen on this pair of animals in Montana.

wait along mouse runs in the meadow, slapping down any careless mice that may come running by, and swallowing them in a gulp. They also kill elk or moose that are weakened after a tough winter, and feed on decaying carcasses of animals, including other grizzlies, that have died. Grizzlies tear apart logs to get at squirrels' hidden stores of nuts and delicately nibble wild berries. They dig up the roots and bulbs of wildflowers and graze on tender grass in meadows.

Like black bears, grizzlies tank up in the fall before

retiring for the winter and may gain close to a hundred pounds of extra fat. While black bears den in natural caves and hollow trees, grizzlies dig their dens in the ground, usually between the strong, supporting roots of a tree. Yellowstone grizzlies dig their dens high up in the mountains, above 8,000 feet in elevation. They choose timbered areas, far from possible human interference. They dig their dens well in advance, sometimes starting as early as the first week in September. It takes several days to dig the long entrance tunnel and the enlarged "bedroom" inside. Many branches must be chewed off nearby trees to build the springy bed on which the bear will lie. In Yellowstone, the den usually faces north so that the entrance becomes covered by snow and is protected from a midwinter thaw which might melt snow on a southern slope. Grizzly denning habits in other areas may be quite different from those in Yellowstone, depending on local conditions. Grizzlies may spend as long as six months in winter sleep, cozily curled up in their dens, lying upon the deep nest of boughs which helps hold in heat and keep the den much warmer than the outside air.

In the springtime, grizzlies come out of their dens and head down into the valleys, where new shoots are pushing up out of the ground. By tracking many grizzlies over a period of years, the Craigheads found that the bears tended to congregate in the valleys in the spring and disperse into the high country for winter denning. Because they are attracted to places where food is abundant, grizzlies often come into contact with one another. They are not so solitary as was once believed. Apparently all the grizzlies within a particular area are acquainted with one another.

Some animal species have definite territories which they occupy. Such animals keep others of their kind away and will not share their private territory. But grizzlies are different. Each bear has its own range through which it moves, its own familiar ground. Some grizzlies stay within a very limited area of a few square miles for their entire lives, but others may move around over hundreds of miles. Males are usually more restless than females and are likely to travel over greater distances. But wherever they live, grizzlies share their home ranges with other bears and do not compete for territories. They accept one another easily. They may even spend a lot of time close to one another.

During spring and fall, when they are especially hungry, grizzlies feed during the day as well as at night. But in summer, they make day beds in the dense timber near the meadows. Often, when the Craighead team was closing in on a bear wearing a radio collar, they surprised other grizzlies as well. As many as thirteen bears were bedded down in one stand of timber. This was tricky business, for a grizzly startled at close range is likely to react by attacking rather than by fleeing. Whenever they were near the bears, the scientists had to make sure that good trees for climbing were nearby.

Grizzlies will also feed peacefully together where food is abundant. An elk carcass, a rich berry patch, a reeking garbage dump, are all places where many grizzlies may congregate to feed. The biggest males, however, have "first dibs" on food when times are lean, and may feed alone for awhile before allowing other grizzlies to share. Among the bears in a particular area, each has its place in the scheme of things. The big males "outrank" the females, and females with cubs outrank lone females. The smaller and younger the bear, the less status it has and the more likely that it will be kept away from food if supplies are limited.

Mating and the Family

Springtime is also mating time. Much of the bear ranking, especially among males, is established at this time, but the challenging and fighting may go on around choice feeding places, like dumps, all season. Big males will challenge one another to fight for the top position. Only one bear can be number one. The challenger walks up, stiff-legged, towards the other male. If the challenged bear does not want to fight, he simply turns his head to one side and backs up slightly. This is his way of saying, "You are top bear." If not, the fight is on. When grizzlies fight, they can inflict painful wounds on one another. Top males usually sport many scars on their faces and necks, and often their ears and jowls are torn. The bears lunge at one another, slapping with their powerful forelegs and biting with their teeth. They may lock jaws and wrestle until one bear gives in. The losing bear lowers his head, turns it sideways, and retreats a step or two. The winner then turns away and walks off. The losing animal never takes advantage of the situation by attacking from behind. Once the fight is over, it is done with. Although the animals come away with gashes, the physical injuries eventually heal. But often the psychological damage done to an older top bear who loses out to a stronger, younger challenger appears to make him age quickly and die soon. More than once, deposed top bears in populations being studied by biologists disappeared and were not seen again.

These spectacular battles often take place while the males are courting, and the top male is likely to end up mating with more females than the others do. Both males and females, however, may mate with more than one other bear during the season.

Like the black bear, the female grizzly carries the undeveloped embryos in her uterus through the summer and fall. Only after she dens for the winter do the embryos become implanted in the uterine wall and undergo their short six- to eight-week development. From one to four baby grizzlies are born in January or Feb-

Big male grizzlies often have scars on their faces from their battles with one another, as this Yellowstone animal does.

These three- to five-month-old grizzly cubs were left in the meadow by their mother while she went off to feed. They are obedient offspring and will stay right where she put them until she calls or returns.

ruary. They are blind, helpless, and hairless. They weigh only about a half kilogram (18 ounces) each. Their small bodies fit into the snug den easily, even as they grow. When the bear family leaves in March or April, the young bears are furry and full of energy, but they weigh only about 2½ kilograms (5 to 6 pounds) each. They are still smaller than the typical human baby at birth.

The mother grizzly takes good care of her cubs. While she looks for food, the young ones romp and play nearby. She does not let them stray far from her side, for they are small enough to make a meal for a bigger bear or possibly other predators. If alarmed, the mother bear gives out a loud huffing call, which brings her youngsters on the run. Any time they do not obey her orders immediately they may be cuffed sharply by their mother. Their lives depend on taking her warnings seriously. Roughly a third of the cubs die from one cause or another from the time they leave their dens the first time until they are 1½ years old.

The grizzly family stays together for a long time. The mother bear nurses her young for many months. Just how long she does so varies from bear to bear and year to year, but usually the cubs nurse for 1½ to 2½ years. The cubs may stay with their mother for some months after weaning, or she may chase them off and force them to go out on their own. The cubs often stay together for several months after their mother makes them leave.

Cubs living in such groups are better off than are single cubs, for they have a higher position on the grizzly social scale. The lowest animal of all is a lone, first-year cub that has lost its mother and is trying to survive on its own.

Surprisingly enough, female grizzlies frequently adopt motherless young. The Craigheads saw several examples of this behavior, which certainly gave cubs a better chance for survival. They also saw cases of female bears which developed "friendships." The females and their cubs would spend most of their time together. In one case, the two females denned only about 1 1/2 miles from one another and spent much of the time before settling in for the winter visiting back and forth. Once, when the researchers disturbed one female, she ran over to the den of her "friend" and gave warning huffs to her before fleeing. In the spring, one of these bears adopted the single cub of the other. Freed from the responsibilities of motherhood, the first female was then able to mate and produce a new litter the next year.

Different Life Styles

Black and grizzly bears are often found living together in the same forests. When two closely related animal species are found together, biologists want to know what differences exist in their life styles. For if the two species lived in exactly the same way, the kind better suited to that life would push out the other species. The differences between grizzly and black bears help explain how they share the forests and tell us some interesting things about their habits and behavior.

While grizzlies often travel into treeless areas in search of food, black bears rarely do. Dr. Gordon Burghart noticed that two black bear cubs he raised in captivity always tended to stay in darker places, out of the bright light. They seemed to feel uncomfortable in open areas, preferring always to stay among the trees. Black bear cubs also spend considerable time climbing trees, and even adult blacks are at home among the branches. Grizzlies, on the other hand, cannot climb as adults. Only the cubs go into the trees, and even then they usually do so only when danger threatens.

Some biologists believe that their habit of leaving the forest and venturing out into open spaces is what makes grizzlies more aggressive than blacks. A bear in the woods can always climb a tree to escape danger. But a bear out in the open has little choice when attacked but to stand its ground and fight. Perhaps this also explains the larger size of grizzlies, for a large bear can defend itself better than a small one. European brown bears, which are smaller than grizzlies, are also less likely to move out of the forest than are grizzlies. Like blacks, these bears may venture onto the tundra to obtain food, but they spend far less time in open areas than do our grizzlies.

Grizzlies also do more digging than black bears. Their claws are longer and wider, enabling them to dig their deep dens in the hillsides. Black bears usually den in hollow trees, caves, or other natural cavities. Their superior digging ability also allows grizzlies to dig out more of their food. Roots, tubers, and termites form an important part of the grizzly diet.

One reason black bears tend to avoid open areas may be the grizzly itself, for large grizzlies may attack small black bears. In parts of Canada where the grizzly no longer lives, black bears may venture out into open areas which they would avoid in grizzly country. Perhaps a new strain of black bears, more adapted to open areas, will develop in these regions free of grizzlies.

Alaskan Brown Bears

Yellowstone grizzlies may be impressively large animals, but Alaskan brown bears are even bigger. A male Alaskan bear may weigh as much as 780 kilograms (over 1,700 pounds) and his body can be 2.8 meters (over 9 feet) long. There are two or three kinds of brown bears in Alaska. The Kodiak bear lives on the Kodiak Islands. Because water separates the islands from the mainland, Kodiak bears cannot breed with mainland bears. Some biologists think that the big brown bears on the mainland are different enough from grizzlies that they, too, should be considered a different subspecies. But grizzlies also live in Alaska and breed with the big brown bears in some areas. So other experts think of them merely as big grizzlies.

Like female Yellowstone grizzlies, Alaskan brown bear females may develop "friendships." Biologists studying bears in the McNeil River area of Alaska watched three females swap cubs over an entire summer. Almost every day the bears would meet and trade cubs. Altogether, there were nine young bears. No female ever went off without at least one cub, and none ever took responsibility for more than six at a time. Unfortunately, the biologists had to leave before finding out how the cubs were sorted out for winter denning.

Alaskan brown bears are especially skillful at fishing. Every year during the salmon run, they gather at streams and rivers to catch fish. McNeil River Falls is an especially good fishing site, and scientists have watched the bears there for several years. Bears return yearly to fish and may stay for more than a month. As many as 25 bears at a time fish at the falls, and they may stand within a few meters of one another. Altogether, 60 to 80 bears visit the falls each year.

Brown bears at McNeil Falls develop a social order similar to those of grizzlies at food sources. One big male is "top bear" and every other bear has its place on the social ladder. The higher the bear's status, the better the fishing spot it can secure. The large males are at the top of the social scale, followed by females with

This Alaskan brown bear has just caught a big salmon in the McNeil River.

cubs. Immature bears are at the bottom of the heap.

The Alaskan bears use several techniques to fish. Sometimes a bear grabs the fish in its mouth, and other times it uses its front paws to pin down its victim. The bears often stand waist-deep in the swift and icy water waiting for fish. Sometimes they watch from a convenient boulder along the shore. The huge animals can be remarkably quick, flying through the air from a boulder and plunging in to grab a passing fish.

Other Brown Bears

Before being exterminated by man in many areas, the brown bear had by far the greatest range of all bears. It was found not only over most of western North America—as grizzlies and Alaskan brown bears—but also throughout most of Europe and Asia and into the Atlas Mountains of Algeria and Morocco. Less than a thousand years ago, brown bears roamed throughout the forested areas of continental Europe. In prehistoric

Despite their large size and stocky bodies, Alaskan brown bears can be very agile, as shown by this animal that is leaping into a river for salmon. MICHAEL LUQUE

NATIONAL ZOOLOGICAL PARK
This European brown bear looks very much like a grizzly.

times, brown bears were found even in the British Isles. Today, however, only isolated populations are found in western Europe, while several Asian populations remain. Some of these brown bears, although considered one scientific species, have very different colors and sometimes different life styles. The Syrian bear, for example, is gray with a white collar, while the Himalayan bear is reddish. Some, like the Japanese bear, have a reputation for bad temper which rivals the grizzly's. But others, such as the small population of about ten animals which survives in the Italian Alps, are extremely shy. Although biologists have found signs that the Italian bears do, in fact, still exist, they are rarely seen. Their diligent avoidance of people is probably the key to their survival.

Brown bears are still fairly common in the mountains of Yugoslavia, Romania, and the Soviet Union. Soviet biologists have studied several brown bear populations and noted that their life style and life history are quite similar to those of our grizzly, except that brown bears in some parts of the U.S.S.R. may not den for the winter. They also spend less time out in the open, and they are less aggressive. The European brown bear lacks the bad reputation of the grizzly for attacking man and livestock.

Four

Giant of the North

The majestic polar bear is the "oddball" of the North American bears. One look and you can see that this bear is different from its cousins, for its creamy white coat sets it off immediately. Its homeland—the barren, cold Arctic ice floes—and its food, chiefly ringed seals, also differ sharply from those of other bears. The polar bear is well-adapted to its special life style. The hairs of its thick coat are hollow, giving extra insulation against the bitter arctic cold, and it has an extra layer of insulating fat under its skin. Its ears are small and rounded like those of other arctic mammals. They have many blood vessels, too, which help keep the ears warm and consequently protect them from freezing.

Polar bear claws are short and sharp, adapted for holding onto prey instead of for digging. And polar bear teeth are sharper and more pointed, as suits a hunter who must tear apart flesh instead of crush nuts and chew leaves.

Polar bears look different enough from brown and

The white coat, short ears, and "Roman nose" of the polar bear (Ursus maritimus) set it apart from its close relatives, brown bears and black bears.

black bears that scientists used to think they belonged to a different scientific genus. While brown and black bears were placed in the genus *Ursus*, the polar was called *Thalarctos maritimus*, the "seashore northern bear." But biologists in recent years have learned a great deal about polar bears, and they have decided that these unique animals actually are very closely related to black and brown bears. Polar bear blood is very similar to that of *Ursus* bears, and polar bears in zoos have actually mated successfully with brown bears, sure proof of their kinship. Biologists now call the polar bear *Ursus maritimus* to show its close relationship with other North American bears.

A Challenging Homeland

Polar bears have become different from their brown bear ancestors because they evolved new characteristics to adapt to their harsh environment. The Arctic is a barren land, populated only by a few kinds of hardy animals. No plants grow in the ice, and winter temperatures plunge down frequently to −40°C (−40°F.) and sometimes even lower.

Polar bears are found all around the Arctic Circle. Their homeland includes areas of five different countries—Norway, Greenland, the Soviet Union, Canada, and the United States. On a flat map of the world, the Arctic is distorted and looks larger than it really is. But actually, the polar basin is quite small. For example, the Arctic Ocean is smaller in area than the continent of Europe, so the polar bear's habitat is really quite limited. Fortunately, the five "polar bear nations" have been cooperating since 1965 on research to learn more about this very special arctic resident, so that it can be protected from extinction.

Biologists once thought that polar bears were eternal wanderers, floating helplessly from place to place with the drifting polar ice. But by marking bears and re-capturing them, scientists have learned that most of them tend to be recaptured in the same area they were tagged. Differences in polar bear skull size and shape in different areas have also supported the idea that there are many separate or localized polar bear populations.

Different populations may have strikingly different life styles, too. While most polar bears stay along the coastline where they can hunt seals, bears in the southern Canadian arctic may even leave the sea and travel into the forest and live more like brown bears. The polar bears which used to live in Labrador were specialized fishermen, like the brown bears in Alaska, while those living on Twin Islands in Hudson Bay are adapted to catching the birds which are common there.

The typical polar bear life style, however, is closely linked with the cycle of seals—especially its favorite food, the ringed seal. Bears must migrate with the seasons to where the seals live. In the fall, when the water

freezes, bears travel out on the ice to its edges. In the summer, they may live on the drifting sea ice, where the seals are plentiful.

The Patient Hunter

Seal hunting takes special talents which the polar bear has developed to an impressive degree. It has several different hunting techniques, depending on the circumstances. The most common method is called "still hunting." Since seals are air-breathing mammals, they must come up for air now and then. They have special holes in the ice where they surface briefly to fill their lungs. The hunting polar bear wanders over the ice until it sniffs out a breathing hole. Then it settles down to wait, sometimes for hours, until the seal gets around to that particular breathing hole. The second it surfaces the bear pounces, slapping the seal with a powerful blow of its paw and grabbing with its teeth. In an instant, the seal is out on the ice, a generous polar bear meal.

Polar bears also stalk their prey. While a seal is resting on the ice, the bear sneaks up, crouching low and

The polar bear has a thick coat which helps it keep warm in the frigid Arctic where it lives. Its large, flat, furry feet help it move confidently over ice and snow.

NEW YORK ZOOLOGICAL SOCIETY

slowly creeping forward, hiding where it can among the blocks of ice. When it gets close enough—about 15 to 30 meters (50 to 100 feet)—the bear rushes across the remaining ice, often surprising the seal before it can slip off into the water. Occasionally, a bear will swim towards its prey, with only its nose above the water. Its body is so well insulated that the icy cold water does not bother it a bit. As the bear nears the seal, it dives down and swims underwater up to the ice, launching its huge body out of the water and onto the ice in a flash.

During the spring, seal mothers give birth to their young in snow covered lairs called "aglos." Although the aglo is covered by as much as two meters (over 6 feet) of snow, the bear can smell the seal pup inside. It then digs out the seal, sometimes crashing down onto the top of the aglos with its front paws to break quickly through the thick overlaying ice and snow.

Polar bears occasionally take other prey—perhaps a walrus calf or a musk-ox hampered by especially deep snow. Birds, eggs, fish, and dead whales also may be eaten. During the summer, polar bears living where plants are found may consume berries and grass like their black and brown relatives, and polar bears have been seen munching on seaweed. Male polar bears may sometimes attack and eat cubs, too. In areas where humans live, polar bears may be pesky scavengers, tearing apart camps and haunting garbage dumps. Bears

around the town of Churchill, on Hudson Bay, cause
real concern. Churchill lies on the migration route.
While passing through, the polar bears feed at the
garbage dump, tip over garbage cans, raid trappers' bait
caches, and may even wander through the city streets
during the autumn, when they are heading back to the
coast and the winter sea ice. On Halloween, Churchill
citizens surround the town with their cars, headlights
brightly lit, in an effort to keep the bears out while the
children go trick-or-treating.

No Water to Drink

The polar bear lives in a land of ice and water, yet
it has no water to drink. Salt water is not suitable for
drinking, and there are heat-balance problems with
eating ice or snow. For many years, naturalists noticed
that male polar bears rarely ate the meat on seal carcasses. They consumed only the skin and the blubber,
leaving the meat for scavenging foxes and birds. This
seemed an odd habit; when the next meal is chancy, why
leave good meat behind? The answer probably has to
do with the way the body uses food. The full-grown
male bear needs little protein for health. Most protein
eaten, therefore, is broken down and chemically altered
to provide energy. But, in order for meat (protein) to be
broken down in the body, large quantities of water must
be taken in. If a full-grown polar bear were to eat all

the meat on a large seal carcass, he would have to take in about 20 to 30 liters (21 to 32 quarts). Even if he could eat enough ice to meet this water need, it would take an enormous amount of energy just to heat the water up to body temperature! The bear is already faced with maintaining a warm body while the air temperature is far below zero. And, whereas the bear must take in water in order to use protein, water is actually released in the process of breaking down fats. So, by eating the blubber and leaving the meat, the male bear is helping keep his body in balance with his surrounding environment.

The seal meat is not wasted, however; female bears and cubs may come along and gobble up the meat left over, for the young cubs need protein for making muscles in their growing bodies. The female's bodies, too, need protein to manufacture milk for the cubs. So, these polar bears can actually use the protein, and they need not drink large quantities of water to rid their bodies of protein waste products.

The Polar Bear Family

Usually, only pregnant female polar bears den for the winter. Other bears stay active through the bitter cold, hunting ceaselessly along the ice edges for seals. The denned females make their cozy homes in snow-banks some time in late fall. Certain land areas are

Polar bears are very strong swimmers and can remain in the water for long periods of time. Cubs begin swimming while still quite small, but are carefully watched by their mothers.

traditional denning sites, and many females may dig their dens in the same vicinity. The den is dug upward through the snow so that warm air is trapped inside. Some females make very elaborate dens with more than one "room," but others have simple dens. Soon after the bear dens, drifting snow covers the opening, and no evidence remains that a bear is inside. As winter rages outside for four to five months, the female stays inside, safe from the biting wind and the bitter cold. Snow is an excellent insulating material, and the body heat generated by the female bear keeps the inside of the den up to 40 degrees warmer than the outside air.

Her cubs are born in late December or early January. Like other bear cubs, they are very small when born. They have only a thin coat of fuzzy white fur and are blind and helpless. But, nourished on their mother's rich milk, they grow quickly. By the time they are about two months old, the cubs can move about and may do a considerable amount of digging in the den. This helps them build the strength they will need when the family breaks out from the den in March or April. From then on, they must follow their mother about on the ice as she searches for food. By this time, however, they have thick, furry coats and weigh about 10 kilograms (22 pounds).

The mother bear hunts baby seals when the family leaves the den, and the cubs stay close to her. They follow behind her as she wanders over the ice, and they watch and imitate her actions. While black bears generally nurse their cubs for less than a year, polar bear mothers may nurse their young for as long as 21 months. Small black bears can easily gather nuts and berries, or munch on grass. But hunting seals requires strength and coordination that only comes with time. When autumn comes again, the young polar bears are the size of large dogs, weighing around 45 kilograms (100 pounds). They may den again with their mother for short periods, but usually the family group hunts most of the winter. As the cubs grow older, they learn bit by bit to hunt for themselves. By the time they are two years old, the cubs begin to have success in "still hunting" seals, but they lack the patience of their mother. At this age, they may wander a kilometer or two from their mother while choosing a hunting site. Unfortunately, females with year-old cubs may be hunted in some areas, resulting in orphaned young that usually cannot survive on their own. Occasionally, female polar bears have adopted the young of slain females, but most orphaned cubs almost certainly starve or are killed by adult bears.

When the cubs are in their second year, the female polar bear may mate. While male bears usually hunt or bed alone, the courting pair may stay together for several days. The cubs must leave, or at least keep their distance from the male.

Female polar bears do not breed until they are four or five years old, and males may first mate at the age of eight. Usually there are two cubs in a litter, but sometimes only one is born; rarely there are three. Because of its years of growth to maturity and its harsh homeland, the polar bear cannot multiply quickly. This makes it a species subject to serious population losses as a result of only minor upsets to its habitat. Whereas the cooperation shown by the five nations to study and manage this bear is encouraging, the increasing human activities related to oil, gas, and shipping, which damage the polar environment, are disturbing to the future of this magnificent northern giant.

Five

The Rest of the Family

While biologists have been working hard to understand North American bears, the other bear species have kept most of their secrets to themselves. This may be changing, however, since the increase in human population the world over is resulting in more and more confrontations between humans and bears. People are also clearing the land and destroying the forests on which bears depend. Bear numbers, like those of too many other wild creatures, are constantly declining. Concerned scientists want to learn more about the world's bears so they can help protect them from extinction.

The Asiatic Black Bear

Slightly smaller than our black bear, the Asiatic or Himalayan black bear lives in forests and brushlands through much of Asia, including Japan and the island of Taiwan. These bears are usually black with a white chin and a white crescent on their chests, but dark

*Himalayan black bears (*Selenarctos thibetanus*) usually have a striking white mark on their chests and a white chin.*

brown individuals are also sometimes seen. While the Asiatic bear lives much like brown and North American black bears, it does not have a prolonged period of winter sleep. During the summer, these bears live in the mountains. They may travel to an elevation of 12,000 feet, coming down to lower, warmer regions in the winter. They make beds of fresh twigs on the ground in the winter and in trees during the summer.

Asiatic black bears are more likely to make trouble with nearby humans than most other bears. They raid herds of sheep, goats, and cattle, and may tear apart beehives in search of honey. There are also many cases on record of these bears killing people.

Females give birth usually to two small cubs and then care for the young until they are almost full grown.

Sun Bears

The Malayan sun bear is the family lightweight, significantly smaller than its cousins. This bear is especially agile in trees, where its small size is an advantage. It is also more active than most other bears. Sun bears in zoos may seem to be quite lazy, for they spend the daytime sleeping and sunbathing. Only at night do they arouse themselves to search for food. These sleek, black bears, with their whitish or orange breast marks and orange or gray muzzles, are quite handsome. Their claws are thick, curved, and pointed and are used to tear up trees in search of bees' nests and insects. Palm trees are also ripped apart for their tender growing shoots, and termite nests provide insect food. Like other bears, sun bears are perfectly willing to fill up on someone else's leftovers and may feed at tiger kills.

While all bears are rather intelligent, captive sun bears have proved their keen minds more than once. One young bear, after watching how the sugar bowl was locked into a cupboard with a key, neatly inserted a claw into the lock, turned it, and opened the cupboard. Another captive would scatter rice from its feeding bowl about, attracting chickens, which it then captured and ate.

A female sun bear has successfully raised cubs at the Fort Worth Zoo several times. While most animals have a fairly predictable gestation period, sun bears do not. This zoo mother gave birth anywhere from 25 to 34 weeks after mating. Her cage was boarded up, and no one disturbed her while her babies were young. She had one cub at a time and cared carefully for each litter. Three or four weeks after birth she would bring her youngster out of the den at feeding time, carrying it by the head in her mouth. While she fed, she held the

*The Malayan sun bear (*Helarctos malayanus*) has short fur and strong claws, which it uses to climb and tear apart trees.*

cub tucked warmly against her chest with one front leg. When the cubs reached a good size, the zoo keepers took them away from the mother and raised them on solid foods.

The Sloth Bear

The sloth bear lives in India, Sri Lanka, and adjacent areas. While the sun bear has a short, sleek coat, the

*The sloth bear (*Melursus ursinus*) has a shaggy coat and strong claws, which it uses to rip apart termite nests. The nostrils of its wide, flexible nose can be closed to keep out termites and bits of debris.* SAN DIEGO ZOO

sloth bear wears long, shaggy, black hair with a prominent white or yellow "necklace" on its chest. It usually weighs over 90 kilograms (200 pounds), but the sloth bear is just as much at home in the trees as its smaller cousin, the sun bear. Sloth bears have a unique and strange way of feeding. Their tongues are long and their lips are flexible. The top front teeth are absent and the roof of the mouth is hollowed out. Termites are the staple food of sloth bears. The bear digs up a termite nest with its heavy, curved claws and sucks in termites with a vacuum-cleaner type action. The sounds it makes while feeding are so loud that they can be heard from many yards away. The sloth bear has a very wide nose for close-up sniffing, but the nostrils can be closed while the animal is feeding so it does not get termites up its nose. Even though it is specialized for eating termites, the sloth bear is also very fond of fruits and honey. Overall, fruit makes up almost half of the sloth bear diet, with honey and insects accounting for the rest.

The mother sloth bear has one or two young at a time. Sometimes the cubs remain with the mother until they are almost full grown. But quite small bears have been seen out on their own, too. When the young bears are frightened, they run to the mother and climb on her back, clinging tightly to her especially long hair.

Unfortunately, sloth bears, like other bears, can get into trouble with humans. While they do not appear to eat the roots of wild plants, sloth bears will invade

Like some other bears, the sloth bear has a handsome white chevron on its chest. Notice its long, curved claws and the bare bottoms of its flat feet.

gardens and dig up cultivated potatoes and yams. Natives also accuse them of eating corn, mangoes, and other cultivated crops. Like other bears, a surprised sloth bear, especially a mother with young, may attack people. As humans invade its habitat in ever-growing numbers, the frequency of such unhappy clashes with humans can only increase, endangering the sloth bear's survival. Even now, it appears to be disappearing over much of its former range.

The Spectacled Bear

Only one bear lives in South America. It is found along the Andes mountains in Venezuela, Colombia, Equador, and Peru. The spectacled bear is quite different from other bears in several ways, and scientists believe that its ancestors are different from those of other bears. Unfortunately, this unusual animal has been little studied, although the New York Zoological Society is sponsoring current research. Besides a light crescent on its neck and lines on its chest, this black or dark brown bear has light circles of fur around its eyes, giving the bear its name.

While populations of spectacled bears apparently have declined greatly in recent years, the wide range of this species may yet save it from extinction. Spectacled bears live in habitats which range from the dry deserts near the coast, up through rain forests and the higher,

The spectacled bear (Tremarctos ornatus) *is the only living survivor of one branch of the bear family. While little is now known of its habits, current field research will reveal more information about this unique animal.*

foggy cloud forests, to treeless areas over 12,000 feet high. Even when surrounded by human settlements, small populations of spectacled bears appear to survive in isolated areas. Unfortunately, native peoples blame the bear for the death of livestock, and spectacled bears are known to have an unfortunate fondness for corn and other crops. The bear is also a favorite with hunters, who can tree it easily with dogs, making it an easy target for a rifle.

Spectacled bears are especially fond of fruit and may settle down for several days in the branches of a fruit-laden tree. The bear builds a platform from the branches, eats all the fruit within reach, and then moves on to a new spot. The nests are usually high up in the tree. In desert areas, spectacled bears eat plants which have water-filled cups at the base of the leaves, probably providing them with enough water so that they need not frequently visit water holes. Spectacled bears also appear to eat many palm nuts. Their teeth and skulls are especially heavy and strong, a feature necessary to deal with this hard, tough food.

The Giant Panda

The familiar black-and-white giant panda, too, is thought to be a bear by many experts. Pandas appear to have a very limited range in western China, an area perhaps only 500 kilometers (about 300 miles) long by 125 kilometers (around 80 miles) wide, although some people claim to have seen pandas outside this region. Giant pandas live high in the mountains, from about 2,600 meters to 4,000 meters (8,500 feet to 13,000 feet) above sea level. The air is always damp and cold there. Pandas have extra thick, coarse outer fur and very dense, oily underfur to protect them from the cold and dampness.

Pandas feed mainly on bamboo shoots. They have the largest broad teeth of any animal in the Carnivora, which they use to crush the tough bamboo stems. Their front paws have an extra "thumb" made up of an elongated wrist bone, which has four muscles to control it. This special "thumb" is used to hold onto the bamboo stems while the panda feeds. Panda mouths and throats have a tough lining to protect them from the coarse bamboo, and the panda stomach is strong and thick-walled, much like a chicken gizzard. Pandas spend most of their time sitting on the ground in the dense bamboo forests, patiently tearing off and chewing the abundant sword bamboo found in their mountainous homeland. Besides bamboo, they are also willing to eat some grass and shoots of flowering plants, as well as small animals on occasion. They may also raid bee hives.

Pandas are basically solitary, except when the mother is bringing up her single cub. During the mating season, both male and female pandas rub the trees with special scent glands on their rear ends which advertise their presence to other pandas. The male panda calls with an eerie haunting call. The female answers with a sheep-like "he-he-he" bleat. Once they have found each other, the panda pair stays together for a few days. Then the male takes off to find another mate, and the female continues her normal routine until she gives birth to

The playful panda (Ailuropoda melanoleuca) *is always a favorite of zoo visitors lucky enough to see one. The hairy soles on the panda's feet help it climb over icy terrain without slipping.*

her tiny, rat-sized cub. The cub grows fast, however, and within a few weeks has developed a pale version of the striking panda coat. The mother panda cares for her young for a year. Then she gives birth to another offspring. Rarely, a female panda will have twins

Pandas mature quite slowly and do not mate until they are six or seven years old.

The Chinese government is very interested in protecting its rare and unique national treasure, the panda. Only government workers who collect live animals for zoos can hunt pandas, and several Chinese zoos have successfully bred the animals. Chinese biologists are studying pandas to learn more about their habits and survival needs so that wild pandas can survive despite the needs of modern civilization.

Six

The Mysteries of Winter Sleep

When a bear enters its winter den, the chemical workings of its body change in amazing ways. No other animals are so perfectly suited to sleeping the winter away as bears. They sleep, but they can awaken almost instantly to defend themselves if danger threatens. Other winter sleepers cannot arouse themselves easily. Bears need not eat, drink, urinate, or have a bowel movement during the entire two-to-five months of winter. To conserve energy, the body temperature of other mammals which hibernate drops very low, and their hearts slow way down. Bears can live through the winter with their hearts only slightly slowed and their temperatures only a bit lower than normal. Scientists are studying bear winter sleep in hopes that, by unlocking its secrets, they can find ways to treat certain human health problems.

The Extremes of Hibernation

The state which biologists call "true hibernation" involves extreme and obvious changes in how the body functions—in its physiology. A true hibernator, such as the Columbian ground squirrel, spends most of the winter in such a deep "sleep" that it seems barely alive. Its body temperature drops from $37\,^{\circ}$C (98.6° F.), which is normal for an active animal, to just a few degrees above freezing. Its heart slows down to just a few beats a minute. The animal stays this way for about a week. Then a strange thing happens. The squirrel's body begins to shiver violently, twitching and shaking wildly. This extreme muscle activity acts to warm the squirrel's body back up to normal active temperature in only about two hours. The squirrel is then fully awake. It can move around normally. It urinates and has a bowel movement. Then, it gradually sinks back into hibernation. This cycle repeats throughout the winter, with the period of "suspended animation" lengthening to about two weeks at the longest. As spring approaches, the "sleep" periods get shorter and shorter again until the animal is back to full activity.

Even when in deep sleep, however, the squirrel is not completely insensitive to its surroundings. If handled roughly, it may try to move. If hurt, it may make little sounds. During an especially cold winter, if the temperature of its burrow drops dangerously close to freezing, the squirrel will arouse and dig deeper so it doesn't freeze to death.

Typical hibernators such as the Columbian ground squirrel cannot live through the winter without getting rid of body wastes. Their bodies have no way of changing their chemistry to allow survival without carrying out the usual body functions. Bears do not slip into as deep a state of "hibernation" as do some mammals. So biologists prefer to use a different term, such as "winter sleep," for the way bears spend the winter. But the winter sleep of bears is actually much more efficient than true hibernation. Bears can wake up fast enough to defend themselves, and may even switch dens if they are very disturbed during the winter. But if you pick up a hibernating ground squirrel, it is completely helpless at first and takes a long time to arouse itself. Also, since bears do not need to eliminate their body wastes during the winter, they can stay in the den and leave no telltale signs of their presence.

Switching Metabolism

The normal chemical functioning of the body is called "metabolism." Certain chemical reactions take place which provide energy and chemical building blocks to the body. In the process, wastes are produced, and these must be eliminated through the urine. Mammals must keep a certain concentration of sugar glucose in the blood. Glucose can be gotten from sugars and starches in the diet, or it can be made from amino acids, the building blocks of proteins. But if the body must make glucose from amino acids, a waste chemical called urea is produced. If too much urea collects in the blood, it can poison the body. The kidneys filter out the urea, and it is eliminated by way of the urine.

When a mammal is not eating, it still must keep the glucose concentration in the blood at a certain level in order to function normally. Since little or no glucose can be made from fat, body proteins must be broken down to keep the proper glucose level. This means that when an animal is not eating, it may become weak very rapidly. Even if the animal is fat it will become weak, for the proteins, which make up the muscles, must be destroyed to keep the body chemistry in balance. An overweight person who tries to lose weight by fasting runs into the same problem. Much of the weight lost during fasting is not fat at all, but rather is vital body protein.

If a bear is deprived of food during the summertime, it loses body protein just like other animals. But when it is in winter sleep, the bear can go for months without eating and not lose protein. How does this happen? As winter approaches, a chemical change somehow occurs in the bear's body. No one knows yet for sure what triggers the change. Possibly, the decrease in day length or in temperature during fall results in a special chemical (a kind of hormone) being released into the bear's bloodstream. This hormone (not yet actually discovered) presumably switches the body cells over to the winter-sleep chemistry. During winter sleep, body proteins are actually broken down. But the urea which results is not eliminated from the body, and it does not accumulate in the blood. Instead, it is somehow recycled so that its nitrogen can be combined with fat-breakdown products to make new amino acids. These amino acids can then be built into new body proteins.

Just how bears are able to recycle urea is somewhat of a mystery, for all mammals, including bears, lack the ability to make direct use of urea. Dr. Ralph Nelson, a doctor who has studied bear winter sleep for several years, believes that an unusual method is used to recycle urea. Dr. Nelson thinks that during winter sleep urea passes through the walls of the intestine. There, bacteria which live in the intestine chemically alter the urea, releasing ammonia. The ammonia then passes into the blood, and the bear's body uses it to make new amino acids.

Sleeping Mothers

The ability of bears to go through winter without losing strength and without eating, drinking, or eliminating wastes gives them a big survival advantage. Mother bears can give birth to their young while protected from enemies. Since body wastes are not released, no telltale odors which might give away the den are produced. If an enemy should find the den anyway, the mother bear can quickly wake up to defend her off-

Baby bears are born in a protected winter den. There they nurse and grow until big and strong enough to survive in the outside world.

spring. Bears thus get a "head start" on raising their families. Since it takes bears so long to grow up to adulthood, this head start is very important.

Another mystery of hibernation is how young, growing bears manage to survive several months without food. Most young mammals, if deprived of protein food, end up with permanent brain damage. Their bodies are unable to function and grow properly without adequate protein. But young bears stop growing and can live perfectly well without proteins for several months. Apparently, some chemical change in their bodies turns off the growth process during hibernation.

Walking Hibernation

Large numbers of polar bears live around the town of Churchill, Canada, during the summertime. Churchill is in the southern part of the polar bears' range, and the bears clearly must struggle to adapt to what are, for polar bears, high summer temperatures. Anything above 10° C. (50° F.) amounts to a heat wave for the heavily furred animals, and they spend much time keeping cool by lying spread out on the cold ground near the shore of Hudson Bay, where cool sea breezes blow. They may dig dens in the ground, reaching down to the ever-cool permafrost layer, and lie there out of the sun.

Biologists have found to their surprise that these polar bears eat very little during the summer. Since seals do not live along the ice-free shores near Churchill, the usual polar bear food isn't even available there. Yet the bears do live there and survive the summer on very little food. This puzzle is only now being looked at by biologists, but Dr. E. W. Pfeiffer of the University of Montana has a hunch that these unusual polar bears are in a state of "walking hibernation" during the summer. Instead of going to sleep in a den like other bears during the cold winter, these bears may be living on the same conserving metabolism during the hot summer.

Keys to Human Problems

If we can understand the mysteries of bear winter sleep, we may be able to deal better with several different human health problems. Kidney disease can be very serious. If the kidneys are not working properly, poisonous urea can collect in the blood. Bears manage to make it through the winter without urinating, yet urea does not accumulate in their blood. Scientists such as Dr. Nelson are developing special diets for human kidney disease sufferers based on the understanding of bear winter sleep. Using these special diets might allow patients to go for longer periods of time before having their blood artificially "cleaned" by a kidney machine.

After spending 20 out of every 24 hours during the fall eating, bears lose their appetites for the winter. Even if awakened and offered food, bears won't eat during the winter, and it takes them awhile to regain their appetites in the spring. If biologists can find out what causes bears to first become so hungry and then so uninterested in food, they might be able to help humans who are seriously overweight. And understanding how bears, especially young ones, can "starve" and remain healthy could bring benefits to the under-nourished people of the world.

If humans are ever to travel to distant planets, many problems need to be solved. One is the tremendous amount of time needed to travel to other worlds. Years aboard a space ship means years' worth of food and water, either brought along or somehow produced along the way. And the potential boredom resulting from years in the small, confined space on board could be a serious problem as well. If we can learn to understand how bears can "tank up" and then sleep for months, waking up strong and healthy, we might be able to develop ways of preparing astronauts for space travel by changing their body chemistry. Perhaps space travelers of the future will be able to eat like kings before takeoff, fattening themselves up for the long voyage ahead. Then they could curl up comfortably and sleep away the time without worrying about eating, drinking, or eliminating body wastes. We have much to gain by learning how other living things, such as bears, solve the problems of living in extreme environments.

Seven

Bears and People

Bears and humans have shared the Earth for thousands and thousands of years. They have used the same land and food sources and have served as food for one another. It is not surprising, then, that bears have been important to people in religion as well as in practical life over the ages. While people the world over have related closely with bears, the minglings of bears with humans in North America are the most familiar to us.

Bears and Indians

Because of their great size, strength, and ferocity, grizzlies held an important place in the legends of many Indian tribes. A Nez Percé legend (this tribe lived in Washington and Idaho) tells of an angry female grizzly who ate an entire Indian band and suffered an understandable stomachache. She went to Coyote for a cure, and at first Coyote did not want to help her. He figured all the animals and Indians would be happier if the griz-

The fact that bears, such as this begging Himalayan black bear, can stand up on their hind legs like humans, has given people a feeling of kinship to these animals.

zly died. His wife then convinced him to take others along and go help the old bear, which recovered with Coyote's help. Coyote then told her she was sick from eating too many chokecherries; he was afraid the people he had brought along would run away if he told the truth. But when they had left, he got ready to run and told the bear the truth. The old grizzly took off after Coyote and chased him through the woods and valleys. Coyote kept changing his shape and eventually tricked the grizzly into trying to cross a bridge made of willows over a river. The great weight of the bear broke the bridge and the animal drowned. The other creatures were finally free of her.

The Shasta and Modoc Indians, who inhabited what is now northern California and southern Oregon, had a beautiful legend telling how they themselves were descendants of the Great Spirit's daughter and her grizzly husband (for details of the legend, see *The Beast That Walks Like a Man*, listed under Suggested Reading).

In those far-off, legendary times, grizzlies stood on their hind legs, spoke their own language, and used clubs for weapons. When the Great Spirit found out that the grizzlies, along with his daughter, had created a new face, he was very angry, for only he had that privilege. He ordered the grizzlies to drop their clubs, walk on all fours, and never speak again. Because these Indians considered grizzlies to be their relatives, they

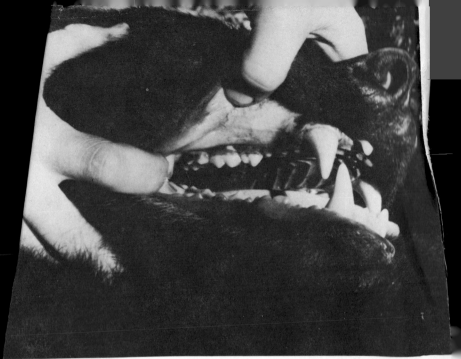

The formidable teeth and claws of the grizzly are powerful weapons it can use against humans.

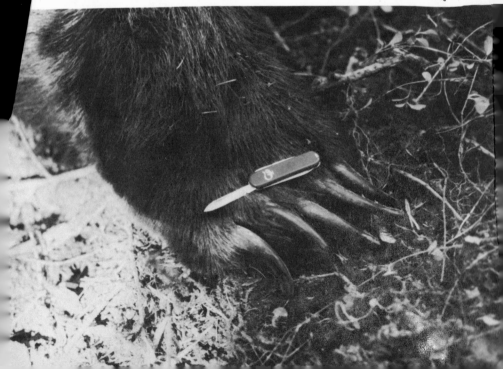

would never kill or disturb them.

California Indians were generally terrified [of griz]zlies. They believed that the big bears were b[ad and] wicked. A particularly bad curse used by the W[intun] Indians was, "May the grizzly bear bite your fa[ce and] head off!" The bears were considered, along with ra[ttle]snakes and stinging plants, as punishments sent do[wn] by their gods to disobedient humans. Some tribes [be]lieved that ghosts of bad Indians ended up in grizz[ly] bodies, to be hated and feared by their former tribes. Wintuns would not eat grizzly meat because they feared taking in these lost souls.

While some tribes would not eat grizzly meat, others did. Grizzly claws were made into necklaces by some tribes. Special, respected tribal members had the privilege of wearing a bear hide among certain tribes. Unfortunately, most California Indians died out before modern anthropology came into being, so much information about bears and Indians has been lost.

For Indians who did hunt bears, a bear hunt was a dangerous undertaking. Lewis and Clark reported that some tribes went through the same rituals before a grizzly hunt as they did before making war on another tribe. Considering that killing a grizzly with bows and arrows and spears is very difficult, and an enraged wounded grizzly is a fearful opponent, such rites are not surprising.

Grizzlies, Lewis, and Clark

Lewis and Clark were the first explorers to describe the grizzly in detail. A couple of others had mentioned it, but Lewis and Clark provided enough scientific information for this new bear species to be recognized. They also were impressed by its ferocity and had many close calls with grizzlies.

Much of the grizzly's bad reputation, which started with Lewis and Clark, is not really deserved. Grizzlies are curious animals and may approach an unfamiliar creature such as a person rather than run away. A grizzly may walk rapidly and deliberately towards a person, standing up on its hind legs for a better look. To the frightened human, this may look like an attack, not a curious approach. If the person is armed, shoots in "defense" and wounds the bear, then the animal will charge out of anger. This sort of thing happened many times during the Lewis and Clark expedition, convincing the explorers that the grizzly was truly a vicious beast. This reputation was kept up by later explorers and trappers and still survives today.

Bull and Bear Baiting

At least since Roman times, human cruelty to animals has shown through in the treatment given bears. In the Roman Colosseum, bears were pitted against gladiators and against other animals. One of the cruelest bear "sports," however, was the bull-and-bear baiting practiced by Spanish settlers in California and continued by later settlers.

The bear was trapped by people on horseback in a fierce battle. One by one the bear's legs were roped as it lunged at its tormentors. When all four legs were roped they were pulled out from under the animal, flattening it helplessly on the ground. The enraged and frightened bear was then dragged off, on a hide pulled by horses or tied to a cart.

The grizzly was then forced into an arena along with a sharp-horned Spanish bull bred for fighting. A hind leg of the bear was linked to a forefoot of the bull by a long leather thong about 16 meters (60 feet) long.

The beasts fought wildly, tearing each other up, with plenty of spilled blood. It was all very exciting for the watching humans and agonizing for the poor animals. Sometimes the bull won by goring the bear. Often the bear won by ripping the bull's tongue to shreds. The victory was short-lived, however, for all a winner had to look forward to was more fights until, it, too, was killed.

Grizzly Adams

While bull-and-bear baiting exploited the fighting nature of the grizzly, an early California pioneer named

James Capen Adams learned to tame grizzlies and make them into loyal companions. Adams lived from 1812 to 1860 and was a professional animal tamer and collector. He captured and sold elk, deer, mountain lions, and other animals as well as grizzlies. But bears were his specialty, and he had many terrible scars to show for his close interactions with these powerful animals.

At least two of his bears became more pets than captives. One, named Ben Franklin, was hand raised by Adams and was very good natured. He even served as a pack animal for Adams and is said to have defended his master against wild animals. Adams raised another bear named Lady Washington, that was also supposed to be a tame and loyal companion. Adams was quite famous during his time, largely because of his grizzlies. He exhibited his "pets," along with other animals, in San Francisco during the 1850s.

Polar Bears and People

Polar bears loom large in Eskimo legend and custom. Many such stories, like stories about other bears, deal with polar bears changing into human form. When Eskimos hunt polar bears, they deal respectfully with their prey. Some Eskimos have special ways to handle the kill to ensure that bear's spirit will not come back to harm them. The hide is removed and placed in a special container ordinarily used for dog food. The bear's soul is pacified by hanging a rope holding a harpoon, some meat and blubber, and pieces of leather around the dead bear's nose. The leather is to make shoes for the bear since it walks so much. If the bear happens to be a female, only the leather, meat, and some seal hide are left for it. All this must remain for five days or more. As the bear is eaten, the bones are carefully gathered and placed on the window sill along with the skull. The skull has to be turned to face the inside.

Polar bear skins make especially soft and warm rugs and boots. They have been prized since Viking times and were given to kings and other important people as special gifts. Polar bear hunting today is severely limited. No hunting is allowed in the Soviet Union and Norway. Whereas the bears used to be hunted for sport from airplanes at one time, now only native peoples may hunt them in Greenland and Alaska for their own use. This use includes making items from the hides to sell to tourists. In Canada, some sport hunting is allowed. Because polar bear hides are valuable, poaching has been a problem at times. But international laws forbidding uncontrolled trade in polar bear hides has helped reduce this problem.

Eight

Living with Bears

Bears bring us face to face with the problems of sharing Earth with other living things. We invade bear country, cut down trees, and build houses. Then we get angry with the "bad" bears which come onto "our" land and eat food from our gardens or tear apart our garbage cans. We set aside special parks where bears are completely protected from human harm and then wonder why they lose their fear of people and invade campgrounds, demanding food and terrorizing campers. Learning to live with bears is not easy. But while learning about the problems and some solutions, we can come to understand much about our effects on the living world as a whole, not just on bears.

As humans destroy more wilderness in Europe, Asia, and the Americas, bears lose out. These large animals require large areas of wilderness in order to live. Most need a variety of habitats—forests and meadows, high country and low—to meet their needs for food and denning sites. Such human activities as logging can de-

This grizzly, foraging at an Alaskan pipeline dump, is learning the bad habit of associating humans and their garbage with food.

stroy vast areas needed by bears for part of the year. And as people move increasingly into bear country, bringing temptations such as corn fields, garbage, and domestic animals, conflicts between bears and humans increase. People come to distrust bears, even hate them, and just want them out of the way.

Some animals, such as coyotes, can reproduce very

fast. The females can breed at a young age and produce large litters. But, as we have seen, bears do not usually breed until they are four to seven years old, and female bears rarely have more than three cubs. They care for the cubs for a long time, too, so that they have new families only every two to four years. If large numbers of bears are killed in one area, it takes many years for the bear population to build up again. Small populations of animals can easily be wiped out by hunters, disease, or unseasonably bad weather. So, whenever bear numbers drop in a particular area, the animals are in danger of being wiped out before the population can be rebuilt.

Learning About Bears

Concerned scientists are studying these problems. They hope to learn enough about bears to save them while keeping harm and inconvenience to people at a minimum. The Bear Biology Association keeps bear specialists in touch with one another, and conferences bring interested scientists together to discuss their research. Many projects are now under way in North America. Scientists are studying the behavior and biology of polar bears near Churchill, Manitoba. They hope to learn what attracts polar bears to come near people and what causes them to attack. This is important work, for while polar bears are not especially aggressive, their great size and strength make them potentially dangerous. As more people move into the Arctic, problems with polar bears are almost certain to increase. Biologists are studying interactions of black bears with people in the Great Smoky Mountain National Park. By learning about attitudes of park visitors to bears, they hope to improve the education of park visitors concerning bears. The more people know, the more they can appreciate the bears, and the better they can avoid problems with them.

Along the U.S.-Canadian border, biologists in the Border Grizzly Project are studying grizzly bears. Dr. Charles Jonkel heads up this ambitious study. The habits and needs of grizzlies along the border are being investigated for 10 years or more, beginning in 1975. This information will help us to better understand the requirements of the grizzly bear and will enable us to minimize unpleasant bear-human encounters.

The Bear's Point of View

Bears are very large and potentially dangerous animals. Many bears are big enough to kill a person with one powerful sweep of a huge front paw. We cannot expect bears to place any particular "value" on human life as we humans do. We can only hope that they will respect us and leave us alone. Bears have no reason to fear humans unless they have had bad experiences with

Black bears are adaptable animals and often lack the natural shyness usually shown by grizzlies. This black bear feels right at home at a human campsite, where it can easily cause plenty of trouble.

them. It must be obvious to a bear that it is stronger and better armed than an unarmed human. If bears learn, as they have at times learned in some of our parks, that humans mean food, then we are sure to have trouble with them. They will naturally be attracted to food sources associated with humans, and if they do not fear people, they will do whatever they can get away with in order to get to the food. If this means chasing off campers, then that is what the bear will do. Such behavior can easily deteriorate into actual attacks on humans. Worse yet, mother bears teach their young this unnatural kind of behavior, and we are stuck with more unafraid and aggressive bears.

The first thing humans must do when learning to live with bears is to accept the animals for what they are— powerful wild creatures with high intelligence and flexible behavior. Bears will feed on wild foods. But if they learn that human foods are easier to get, naturally they will go for them. Fortunately, bears have at least some natural aversion to having showdowns with humans. During the entire time they were studying grizzlies in Yellowstone, the Craigheads and their co-workers never had to shoot to protect themselves from the bears. They climbed plenty of trees, but usually the bears they encountered ran away rather than trying to attack.

Why Do Bears Attack?

If a bear does attack someone, there is almost always an understandable cause. A hungry bear accustomed to associating humans with food instead of danger is rummaging around a campsite and mauls a person in the process. A female with cubs is surprised by a hiker who approaches downwind and sees the hiker as a threat to her family. Actually, many bear "attacks" are really bluffs. But who wants to stick around when a bear charges, rears up, huffs a warning, and slaps the closest tree trunk with a powerful clawed paw? After such a warning charge, most bears will turn away and leave the person alone.

Black bears, although they have a better reputation than grizzlies, sometimes do attack people. A very few cases are even known of black bears actually regarding humans as prey. So any bear in the wild should be treated with the respect due such a large, powerful, unpredictable animal.

Yellowstone Misunderstandings

When humans refuse to accept bears for what they are, trouble results. The history of bears in Yellowstone Park provides several sad lessons in bear-human relationships. Yellowstone Park was created in 1872 and

In parks where they are protected, black bears can quickly associate roads with humans and food. Strict policies forbidding the feeding of bears in parks are important.

soon developed a reputation as a haven for bears. Hotels and campgrounds were set up on the meadows which bears visited, and garbage dumps near the hotels attracted large numbers of bears. The dumps made scavengers out of the grizzlies and decreased their caution toward humans. During the early days, when people arrived by trains and stayed at the established hotels, there were few problems. But after 1930, when roads were built and more and more visitors drove into the park, bear problems increased. Black bears, which lose their reservations about humans more easily than grizzlies, quickly learned to beg along the roadsides. They became a major attraction and caused huge traffic jams, as people piled out of their cars to feed and photograph the bears. The bears became more and more "tame," stood up on their hind legs to beg, and sometimes even took food right from people's hands. The people began to forget that the bears were actually wild animals interested only in food.

Meanwhile, the park hotels competed for customers by "improving" their grizzly attractions. Bleachers with floodlights were set up so people could sit and watch the bears scrounge in the dumps. At times, garbage was even sorted for the bears and edible parts put on tables so that people could see the bears better. Especially tasty tidbits, such as bacon, were offered along with the garbage to encourage the bears to fight over the food.

Not only did all this nonsense encourage the bears to associate food with people and to lose their natural shyness, it also brought more and more people to the park expecting to see bears. And the more people there were in the park, the greater the chances of trouble with the bears, especially when the people looked upon them as a tourist attraction instead of as wild, strong, unpredictable animals.

This went on until 1941, when the park closed the dumps to public viewing. Then, during World War II, several dumps were closed. This action forced both black and grizzly bears into the campgrounds to look for food. Fifty-four black bears and 28 grizzlies were shot in the process. But several dumps were still left open near campgrounds, and black bears were still begging by the roadsides.

Finally, in 1960, the Park Service changed its policy. Realizing that the bears had become unnaturally dependent on humans and unnaturally bold around people, park officials decided to crack down on the problem bears. From then on, if people wanted to see the bears, they would have to see them in their natural surroundings, not at dumps, along roadsides, or in campgrounds. People were discouraged from feeding roadside bears. Problem bears were drugged and transported as far away from tourist attractions as possible. The Craigheads, who had begun their Yellowstone studies in 1959, cooperated in tranquilizing and transporting the problem bears.

During the 12 years of their studies, the Craigheads worked with some 900 individual bears. They carefully plotted the movements of the grizzlies and determined the lifetime range of many. Their findings showed that bears denned in the remote high country but gathered around the lush valleys in the spring and summer to feed. In the fall, many of the bears moved around again, traveling to fall feeding areas. Although they did not tag and track every grizzly in the park, they felt that their studies clearly showed that most Yellowstone grizzlies eventually showed up at the garbage dumps.

In 1967, the Park Service decided to close the Yellowstone garbage dumps and to do it quickly. The Craigheads feared this approach would lead to trouble. The bears were used to getting food at the dumps. If they suddenly were not there, the bears might wander into campgrounds and cause trouble in their search for food. The Craigheads felt the dumps should be gradually phased out so the bears could get used to the situation gradually. They felt that carcasses could be left for bears in areas away from campgrounds. The bears' sensitive noses would lead them to the carcasses, and they would learn bit by bit to stay away from the old dumps and from the campgrounds.

Park Service officials ignored these recommendations. Partly because of public pressure (two women were killed by grizzlies in Glacier Park in 1967), the Park Service stuck to its decision to close the dumps and close them fast. They forgot what happened in the 1940s when dumps were closed and bears invaded camp-grounds. But when the amount of refuse food left at one dump was greatly reduced in 1968, bears began to show up in nearby campgrounds in record numbers. For example, 33 "bear incidents" were reported in 1966, nine in 1967, and a whopping 84 in 1968 at one campground. During the closing of the dumps, many bears lost their lives, and the Craigheads feared for the future of the entire Yellowstone population, since they believed all bears eventually came to the dumps.

The Craigheads and park officials kept disagreeing over how to manage the park bears. Eventually, the controversy reached the point where the Craigheads felt forced to leave and abandon their studies in 1971. The conditions placed on any agreement with the Park Service were impossible to accept. The whole incident was very unfortunate, for much of the value in a long term study of wildlife was lost. Since they knew the personal history of so many bears, the Craigheads could have learned a great deal about the social structure of the Yellowstone grizzlies. Did most female bears tend to remain in the area where they were born? Did most young males wander away to new homes? When female bears associated with one another and adopted cubs, were they dealing with their own daughters and sisters or with unrelated bears? Such questions and many more can only be answered by long-term studies, since grizzlies take so long to grow up and reproduce. Meanwhile,

JOHN CRAIGHEAD

This is a portrait of the grizzly, Marian, the first grizzly bear to be tracked by radio. The Craigheads followed Marian's activities for eight years. Eventually she was shot by a park ranger, while trying to protect her cub, after the Craighead studies had ended.

park officials claim that the Yellowstone grizzly population has stabilized at a healthy level and that the animals are not in danger of dying out. Some biologists, including the Craigheads, doubt the official figures. Others believe they are accurate.

Keeping the Bears

How can we preserve our bears without endangering humans who come into contact with them? This question becomes more and more urgent as more people visit the parks and camp there. A few people have been killed by grizzlies in parks, and black bears have sometimes attacked park visitors. How can we minimize the dangers?

Many animal lovers believe that bear hunting, especially of grizzlies, should be banned. They feel that there are too few grizzlies left already and that hunting will kill off too many of those that remain. Others believe that hunting is legitimate recreation, that it tends to eliminate the bolder and more dangerous bears, and that it teaches bears to avoid humans.

It is especially important to keep bears from learning to associate people with food. Campers should cook away from where they sleep. They should keep their food away from their tents and, if possible, out of reach of the bears. Food odors should be kept to a minimum by wrapping food thoroughly or by keeping it in coolers and other tight containers. Garbage should be kept away from campgrounds, too, and people who feed bears should be fined. If you feed a bear, you may not get hurt. But you are teaching the bear bad habits which may end up hurting someone else.

Campgrounds and trails in parks should be located away from areas where bears tend to concentrate. Unfortunately, present campgrounds and trails were located by engineers, not by wildlife biologists. Many of them are in the worst possible places. Narrow canyon paths, for example, are used by both bears and people. Humans like open meadows, but so do the bears. Campgrounds and trails for people should be located away from concentrations of such popular bear food as huckleberries, mountain ash, and glacier lilies. At times of year when bears congregate in certain areas, these places should be closed to humans.

Any person hiking in bear country should do whatever possible to avoid surprising bears. Loud talking or singing helps, as do bells which jingle loudly while on walks. If a bear hears someone coming, chances are it will turn quietly away and leave. But if a bear is suddenly surprised at close range, it may attack. If humans can learn to respect bears and to be cautious when visiting bear country, we can share our forests and mountains with these magnificent creatures of the wild.

Suggested Reading

Books

Bernadine Bailey, *Wonders of the World of Bears* (Dodd, Mead, N.Y., 1975).

Bears and Other Carnivores (Silver Burdett, Morristown, N.J., 1977). A Time-Life book.

Susannah Cook, *A Closer Look at Bears and Pandas* (Watts, N.Y., 1976).

Frank C. Craighead, Jr., *Track of the Grizzly* (Sierra Club Books, San Francisco, 1979). Account of the Craighead's research, including a history of the Yellowstone controversy from the Craighead's point of view.

Thor Larsen, *The World of the Polar Bear* (Hamlyn, N.Y., 1978). Book by a polar bear expert, with many fine color photographs.

Harold McCracken, *The Beast That Walks Like a Man* (Houghton Mifflin, Boston, 1955).

Dorothy H. Patent, *Raccoons, Coatimundis, and Their Family* (Holiday House, N.Y., 1979). Includes information on the giant panda, which many experts think is a bear.

R. Perry, *The World of the Polar Bear* (Cassell, N.Y., London, 1966).

Margaret Rau, *The Giant Panda at Home* (Knopf, N.Y., 1977).

Andy Russell, *Grizzly Country* (Knopf, N.Y., 1968).

Bill Schneider, *Where the Grizzly Walks* (Mountain Press, Missoula, MT, 1977). Account of the problems of conserving grizzlies and grizzly habitat.

Joe Van Wormer, *The World of the Black Bear* (Lippincott, N.Y., 1966).

Magazine Articles

Fred Bruemmer, "Never Trust Nanook," *International Wildlife*, July-Aug. 1979. About polar bears, especially near Churchill.

Christopher Cauble, "Glacier's Bad News Bears," *National Wildlife*, June-July, 1979. About grizzlies in Glacier Park.

Frank C. Craighead, Jr., "Trailing Yellowstone's Grizzlies by Radio," *National Geographic*, Aug. 1966.

————, "They're Killing Yellowstone's Grizzlies," *National Wildlife*, Oct.-Nov., 1973.

John Craighead, "Studying Grizzly Habitat by Satellite," *National Geographic*, July 1976.

Frank C. and John Craighead, "Knocking out Grizzly Bears for Their Own Good," *National Geographic*, Aug. 1966.

Allan L. Egbert and Michael H. Luque, "Among Alaska's Brown Bears," *National Geographic*, Sept. 1975.

Bill Gilbert, "The Great Grizzly Controversy," *Audubon*, Jan. 1976.

Thor Larsen, "Polar Bear: Lonely Nomad of the North," *National Geographic*, April 1971.

Jack W. Lentfer, "Solitary Sea Bear," *Oceans*, Sept.-Oct. 1979.

Michael R. Pelton and Gordon M. Burghardt, "Black Bears of the Smokies," *Natural History*, Jan. 1976.

Bill Schneider, "Will this Grizzly Attack?" *National Wildlife,* Feb.-Mar. 1977.

Peter Steinhart, "Getting to Know Bruin Better," *National Wildlife,* Aug.-Sept. 1978. About bear biologists and their studies.

Savva M. Uspenskij, "An Olive Branch for the Polar Bear," *International Wildlife,* May-June 1974.

Index

adoption of cubs, 50
aglo, 64
ammonia, 89
Arctic, 60, 91

bacteria, 89
bamboo, 82
Bear Biology Association, 105
bear trees, 36
Bears, attacks on humans, 109;
colors of, 15-16, 18-19, 25, 41,
71-73, 73, 77, 79; family life
of, 23-24, 28-35, 49-50, 53, 66-
70; food of, 12, 16, 17, 33,
41-43, 45, 61, 63-66, 73, 77, 79,
80-81, 82; life span, 35; milk
of, 28; in parks, 108-116; size
of, 15, 29, 41, 49, 52; studying, 26-27, 38-41; traits of, 15
bears and humans, 13-15, 94-117;
conflicts between, 103-105
black bear, American, 16, 18-19,
25-36, 43, 50-52, 69, 106, 107,
109, 110, 111, 112; Asiatic, 22,
71-73, 95
blood glucose, 87-88

Border Grizzly Project, 106
brown bear, 23, 37; Alaskan, 14,
15, 18, 19, 52-54, 55; Asian, 18;
European, 18, 51, 55-57; Himalayan, 56; Italian, 57; Japanese, 56-57; Syrian, 56; *see
also* grizzly bear
bull and bear baiting, 99-100
Burghardt, Dr. Gordon, 51

camping in bear country, 116-117
Carnivora, 21; cat group, 22; dog
group, 22
cave bear, 22-23
China, 81, 84
Churchill, Manitoba, 65, 91, 105-
106
claws, 27, 41, 52, 58, 73, 75, 77,
78, 98
coyotes, 104-105
Craighead, Drs. Frank and John,
37-41, 43, 50, 108, 112-116
cubs, 28-30, 46-50, 68-69, 83

delayed implantation, 24, 46
denning, 33-34, 43, 66-68, 113

differences between black and grizzly bears, 41, 50-52

ears, 15, 58, 59
Eskimos,101-102
Etruscan bear, 22
evolution, 21-23

fasting, 88
fighting, 46, 47
fishing by bears, 53-54
"friendships" in bears, 50, 52
fur, 15, 58, 59, 62, 81-82, 102

Glacier Park, 113
Great Smoky Mountain National Park, 106
Grizzly Adams, 100-101
grizzly bear, 18, 37-52, 94, 98, 99, 100, 106, 111-116; California, 37, 100; reputation of, 99
ground squirrel, Columbian, 86-87

hearing, 28
hibernation, true, 85-87; walking, 91-92; *see also* winter sleep
Himalayan black bear; *see* black bear, Asiatic
home range, 36, 44
Hudson Bay, 91
hunting of bears, 69, 101-102, 116

Indians, California, 97; Modoc, 96; Nez Percé, 94; Shasta, 96; Wintun, 97

Indian legends, 94-97

Jonkel, Dr. Charles, 106

kidney disease, 92
Kodiak bear, 52

Lewis and Clark, 99

Marian, 115
mating, 34-35, 45, 69-70, 82
metabolism, 65-66, 87-89
miacids, 22

Nelson, Dr. Ralph, 89, 92

panda, giant, 20-21, 81-84; lesser, 20, 21
Pfeiffer, Dr. E. W., 91
play, 32-33
polar bear, 4, 15, 16, 18, 23, 58-70, 101-102, 105-106; diffferences from black and brown, 58-60; life styles, 61; range, 60-61

radio collars, 40
Roman Colosseum, 100

seals, 63-65
seal hunting by polar bears, 63-64
sense of smell, 28
sloth bear, 16, 76-79
social rank, 45-46, 50, 53-54
space travel, 93
spectacled bear, 12, 16, 17, 79-81
"still hunting," 63, 69
sun bear, 15, 73-76

tails, 15
teeth, 98
termites, 77
tongues, 77

urea, 87-88, 89

vision, 28

winter sleep, 34, 43, 85-93; differences from true hibernation, 87

Yellowstone Park, 37-41, 43, 108, 109-116